breat

Created

participant's guide

Shawna Songer Gaines

BEACON HILL PRESS
OF KANSAS CITY

Copyright © 2015 by Beacon Hill Press of Kansas City

Beacon Hill Press of Kansas City
PO Box 419527
Kansas City, MO 64141
www.BeaconHillBooks.com

ISBN 978-0-8341-3365-5

Printed in the
United States of America

Cover Design: J.R. Caines
Interior Design: Sharon Page

10 9 8 7 6 5 4 3 2 1

Contents

How to Use this Participant's Guide

Thank you for joining us on this journey through *Breathe: Created*. As you discover what God has to say to you in this study, we would like to give you a new tool to help you understand the Bible. This tool is called biblical theology.

Biblical theology is a lens for reading Scripture that is set to look for the big story that God is telling throughout history. Biblical theology places scripture in conversation with scripture and assumes that every book is telling a different perspective of the same story, a story which the Church is still telling today!

As we study Scripture through the lens of biblical theology, we use another tool: hermeneutics. Don't be intimidated by the big word—hermeneutics is simply a way to explain or interpret Scripture. The three hermeneutical questions we will ask in each lesson are:

1. What do you learn about the character of God?

2. What do you learn about what God is up to in our world?

3. How do you see this God at work in the world still today?

These three questions help us reflect on each scripture passage. The questions that we ask reveal the lens with which we see God and read scripture. These questions assume at least three things:

1. God is the primary character in Scripture.
2. God's actions are consistent with God's character.
3. God's character never changes, so we can look for God to be at work today with the same goals we see in Scripture.

As we study Scripture, we must also understand its inspiration. We believe that Scripture is the inspired word of God. In fact, we believe that it is God breathed. While it is important that we study and dig into Scripture to learn more about who God is and what God is up to, it is just as important that we always approach Scripture in the power of the Spirit. That is why this participant's guide includes guides for prayer and meditation. These practices help to open us up to the Spirit who breathed into the biblical writers and breathes inspiration and revelation into God's people of every generation.

Finally, we need to understand the echoes from scripture to scripture. Because Scripture is breathed by the Holy Spirit, there are echoes of themes that reveal God's character. Even though there is an incredible variety of Biblical genres and authors, and even though the Bible was written over a span of roughly 1,500 years, the same images of God's character ring throughout the pages of Genesis to Revelation. The creation story echoes across Scripture because it reveals something of God's character that is vital to our relationship with our Creator.

As you work through this study, you may want to refer to this introduction from time to time to help you recall the tools of biblical theology. Blessings to you and may God do a great work in you as you study *Breathe: Created.*

1 *Create*

∾ INTRODUCTION

Creation is so much more than rocks and trees, birds and insects. Creation reveals the character of God. God was, is, and always will be creative and creating. That is why we see echoes of the creation story from Genesis to Revelation; God can't stop being our Creator.

God is the only Creator. "There is nothing new under the sun," and our attempts at creativity are simply rearranging the things God has made. God is the only one who can make something out of nothing.

God's creation story is an intimate revelation of God's involvement in our world. God doesn't assemble creation from a box; God breathes creation into being. Scripture tells us God's Ruach, or Spirit, was hovering over the dark nothingness, breathing life where there was none.

There is nothing in all creation that God hasn't made, named, and ordered. Even darkness, which can seem chaotic and scary, has been put in its place by God. The next time you feel the waters of darkness and chaos closing in around you, take a deep breath and remember the Spirit of God is giving you life and calling you to worship. As long as you are breathing and worshiping our Creator God, you are fit for your purpose in this world. You are a good creation. No one else's opinion of you defines your goodness, not even your own negative view of yourself. As you take that deep breath, let God remind you that you are pleasing to your Creator.

∽

∽ BREATHE IN THE WORD

Read each scripture passage and answer the question after the passage.

Genesis 1:1: How does thinking of heaven and earth being part of one creation change how you see the world?

Genesis 1:2-5: What does it mean to you that out of darkness, God created light?

Genesis 1:6-10: How do you respond to the fact that not only does God create, but God also has a plan and a place for each creation?

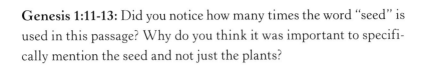

Genesis 1:11-13: Did you notice how many times the word "seed" is used in this passage? Why do you think it was important to specifically mention the seed and not just the plants?

Genesis 1:14-19: Did you notice that God already created light (v. 3), before creating the sun and stars? Do you think that's significant? If so, why?

Genesis 1:20-25: What does God's command to the creatures "be fruitful and increase in number" tell you about God's plan for creation?

⌒∽ PRAYER

Creator God,
Breathe the Word of life into me.
Open my eyes to see beyond the words on the page.
Enliven my imagination to grasp the bigger story
you are still writing today.
May I surrender to the work you are doing
throughout history.
Right now, in this holy moment, create me anew.
In the name of Jesus and in the power of the
Holy Spirit.
Amen

Remember that we are looking at the Bible through the lens of biblical theology, asking God to open our eyes to the Spirit's echoes in scripture as we consider passages not as solitary stories but as open conversations that thread throughout the entire Bible. Remember, too, that we also bring ourselves to the conversation, and the way we see God affects how we read God's story. Ask God to open your eyes and your heart as you consider this week's passage.

{ Genesis 1:1-25

What do you learn about the character of God?

What do you learn about what God is up to in our world?

How do you see this God at work in the world still today?

∽ EXERCISE

My breaths each minute:	
Minutes per hour:	x60
Hours I am awake:	x
Breaths per day:	=
Breaths given to God per day:	/10=
Divide by breaths per minute:	/
Minutes to offer to God:	=

How many times do you breathe in a day? Try to find out. Count your breaths for one minute. There are sixty minutes in every hour and with twenty-four hours in a day that makes 1,440 minutes. God asks us to give a tenth of all we have back to the Lord. Have you ever thought of giving a tenth of every breath back to God? Let's say you spend eight hours sleeping. That brings us down to 960 minutes a day. How many breaths is that for you? Your challenge this week is to spend one day offering one in ten of your God-given breaths back to God. That is about ninety-six minutes. That can look like a lot of different things.

Here are a few ideas:

- Tell someone about what God has done for you.

- Sing praises to God on your way to work and while you run errands.

- Go for a prayer walk.

- Read God's word out loud by yourself or with a friend.

What are your ideas for giving your breath back to God?

ɷ REMEMBER

- God is the main character of this story and every story in the Bible.

- God's Spirit is intimately involved in the world, breathing new life into God's creation.

- Creation is the space God gave us for worship—that means the whole world is God's sanctuary, not just the church.

- God has even ordered the darkness and infuses each new day with God's life-giving breath, so we can just breathe!

- If we are worshiping our Creator, we are fit for the purpose for which God made us.

捴 MEDITATE

Imagine yourself as a living house. God comes in to rebuild that house. At first, perhaps, you can understand what He is doing. He is getting the drains right and stopping the leaks in the roof and so on: you knew that those jobs needed doing and so you are not surprised. But presently he starts knocking the house about in a way that hurts abominably and does not seem to make sense. What on earth is He up to? The explanation is that He is building quite a different house from the one you thought of—throwing up a new wing here, putting an extra floor there, running up towers, making courtyards. You thought you were going to be made into a decent little cottage: but He is building a palace. He intends to come and live in it Himself.[1]

—C. S. Lewis

捴 NOTES

_____

_____

_____

_____

_____

_____

2 | *Image*

෨ INTRODUCTION

You are made in the image of God. In fact, out of all creation God chose human beings—male *and* female—to be the image bearers of God, to reveal to the world who the Creator is. When it comes to creating humans, God does something new. Similar to how the other creatures were made, God forms Adam from the dirt, but what we haven't seen before is what comes next—God breathes into Adam's nostrils, fills Adam with God's life-giving *Ruach* (Spirit). To be human is no second-class fate. In addition to being image bearers, God also chose us to rule over the rest of creation, to re-enact God's relationship with us by how we treat the world.

In order to provide an adequate picture of God to the world, we need both men and women who are living out their purpose—pointing creation back to the Creator. And because God is bigger than any one kind of human, it is only through the vast expanse of a diverse humanity that we can begin to represent the fullness of God.

However, though God designed us with a specific purpose, we have the freedom to choose whether we will follow God and participate in the plan of creation, or turn away from God (sin) and choose to dismantle what God has made.

༄

ᔕᖇ BREATHE IN THE WORD

Read each scripture passage and answer the question after the passage.

Genesis 1:26-27: Did you notice that God created *both* male and female to represent God's image? What does this mean to you? What does this reveal about God?

Genesis 1:28-31: How do you think God intended humans to rule over the earth? What do you think this looks like for us in today's world?

Genesis 2:1-3: Did you notice that while the first six days of creation end with "And there was evening, and there was morning," the seventh day account doesn't? What do you think this signifies?

.

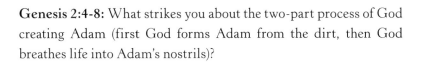

Genesis 2:4-8: What strikes you about the two-part process of God creating Adam (first God forms Adam from the dirt, then God breathes life into Adam's nostrils)?

Genesis 2:9-17: What stands out to you about God's beginning plan for Adam? Does anything surprise or confuse you?

Genesis 2:18-25: How is Eve's creation story different from Adam's, and all the other creatures? What does this tell you about how God sees women?

∽

PRAYER

> *Creator God,*
> *Breathe the Word of life into me.*
> *Open my eyes to see beyond the words on the page.*
> *Enliven my imagination to grasp the bigger story*
> *you are still writing today.*
> *May I surrender to the work you are doing*
> *throughout history.*
> *Right now, in this holy moment, create me anew.*
> *In the name of Jesus and in the power of the Holy*
> *Spirit,*
> *Amen*

We are looking at the Bible through the lens of biblical theology, asking God to open our eyes to the Spirit's echoes in Scripture as we consider passages not as solitary stories but as open conversations that thread throughout the entire Bible. Remember, too, that we also bring ourselves to the conversation, and the way we see God affects how we read God's story. Ask God to open your eyes and your heart as you consider this week's passage.

18   Image

∾

{ # Genesis 1:26—2:25

What do you learn about the character of God?

What do you learn about what God is up to in our world?

How do you see this God at work in the world still today?

∽

∽ EXERCISE

You are a visible snapshot of the invisible God. Does that make you squirm? Especially when you think of photos of yourself that you don't like? As women, we tend to carry a very strict set of criteria about what constitutes "looking good," so it can be difficult to believe that the faces and bodies we deem inadequate (ours!) could possibly reflect a good and brilliant Creator. Let's try an experiment to better understand how we visually represent God to others.

- Find a photo of yourself that your friends and family love, but that you wish never existed.

- Now, find a photo of a friend or family member that you love, but that person doesn't like.

- Lay these pictures side by side, and then consider the second image (the one of the other person). What do you love about this picture? What does this picture reveal about this person? How does this image reflect God?

- Now, consider the picture of you through the eyes of your loved ones. What do they love about this picture of you? What do you think they see revealed about you in this picture? How might this image reflect God?

You can do this exercise by yourself, or ask a friend or family member to do it with you.

⌒⌒

⌒ REMEMBER

- To be made in God's image is to represent God to the world.

- Both male and female represent the image of God. It takes men and women walking through life side by side to be God's image in the world.

- God created us to be creative. God created through words, and words are powerful. We can choose to create or destroy with our words.

- Humans were taken from the earth and then told to tread over the earth; someday we will all return back to the earth. Let us tread lightly as we follow in God's footsteps—creating rather than destroying.

> When God created Eve, she was not an afterthought or subpar creation. She was formed to capture the fullest expression of our rescuer God—a representation of God's character as the very present help in times of trouble.

∽

It has seemed to me sometimes as though the Lord breathes on this poor gray ember of Creation and it turns to radiance— for a moment or a year or the span of a life. And then it sinks back into itself again, and to look at it no one would know it had anything to do with fire, or light. . . . Wherever you turn your eyes the world can shine like transfiguration. You don't have to bring a thing to it except a little willingness to see. Only, who could have the courage to see it? . . . Theologians talk about a prevenient grace that precedes grace itself and allows us to accept it. I think there must also be a prevenient courage that allows us to be brave—that is, to acknowledge that there is more beauty than our eyes can bear, that pre-cious things have been put into our hands and to do nothing to honor them is to do great harm. And therefore, this cour-age allows us . . . to make ourselves useful.[1]

—Marilynne Robinson

∽ NOTES

_____

_____

_____

_____

_____

_____

3 | *Promise*

◎ INTRODUCTION

The story of creation isn't just found in the first two chapters of Genesis. We can see its echoes throughout the Bible. At first glance, the story of the flood may seem like a story of destruction. But, consider what has already been revealed of the character of God. God is creative, not destructive. Let this revelation give you fresh eyes to see this story.

Sin makes nothing out of something; it is the most uncreative act we can take. If sin is not only uncreative but actively destructive, then the natural consequence for those who sin is death and destruction. But though God has every right to wipe the world out in anger and start over again from scratch, God grieves. And in God's sorrow over humanity, we glimpse a better picture of the Creator. Rather than a distant designer who's just experimenting with various ideas, ready to move on at a moment's notice, we see an intimate Creator who lovingly chooses to save a remnant—and stick with the original creation plan.

Suddenly, amid the chaos of the floodwaters we begin to see a story of re-creation. We see the *Ruach* of God blow over the waters and where before there was death, we begin to see new signs of life. God still has a plan and a future in mind for creation, and God is willing to do whatever it takes to help humans fulfill their purpose. God even makes a promise to humankind to that effect.

∽ BREATHE IN THE WORD

Read each scripture passage and answer the question after the passage.

Genesis 6:1-7: What does the fact that God was grieved by humanity's choices reveal about God's character?

Genesis 6:8-22: Following God's statement in verse 7, were you surprised by how the story shifts in verse 8? What do you learn from God's relationship with Noah?

Genesis 7:1-16: How do you read this passage differently if instead of seeing it as a story of destruction, you see it as the start of a re-creation story?

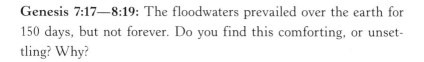

Genesis 7:17—8:19: The floodwaters prevailed over the earth for 150 days, but not forever. Do you find this comforting, or unsettling? Why?

Genesis 8:20—9:7: How does this reflect the original creation story? Has anything changed? Do you have a clearer image of God after reading this re-creation story?

Genesis 9:8-17: This is the first time in the Bible that we see God make a promise. What strikes you about what this promise reveals about God's character and God's plan for creation?

∽ PRAYER

Creator God,
Breathe the Word of life into me.
Open my eyes to see beyond the words on the page.
Enliven my imagination to grasp the bigger story
you are still writing today.
May I surrender to the work you are doing
throughout history.
Right now, in this holy moment, create me anew.
In the name of Jesus and in the power of the Holy
Spirit,
Amen

Remember that we are looking at the Bible through the lens of biblical theology, asking God to open our eyes to the Spirit's echoes in scripture as we consider passages not as solitary stories but as open conversations that thread throughout the entire Bible. Remember, too, that we also bring ourselves to the conversation, and the way we see God affects how we read God's story. Ask God to open your eyes and your heart as you consider this week's passage.

{ ## Genesis 6:1—9:17

What do you learn about the character of God?

What do you learn about what God is up to in our world?

How do you see this God at work in the world still today?

⌒ EXERCISE

Think about a time in your life when everything seemed chaotic and destructive. Can you remember how it felt impossible for anything to change, for anything good to come from the mess? As humans, our tendency is to move on and start over, to try something else entirely. But God appears to have a different approach; God tends to stick with the mess—and create again from the chaos. Let's try to visualize this.

- Find a scrap of paper (if you have a coffee filter, even better). Write down a word or phrase that describes that chaotic time in your life.

- Find an empty pot/jar/can/mug and fill it with dirt. (If your container doesn't have a hole in the bottom, put a layer of rocks and/or sand at the bottom before adding the dirt.)

- Bury the scrap of paper deep in the dirt—and with it, bury that dead and lifeless time of your life.

- Now, plant a few flower seeds about an inch deep in the dirt. (Marigolds, zinnias, cosmos, or dianthus are good choices because they germinate in less than a week.)

- Add a moderate amount of water and set your container in a spot where it receives sunlight. (Over the next few days/weeks keep the soil moist, as needed.)

Now, watch what God can create out of your destructive chaos.

∽

∾ REMEMBER

- Sin is the most uncreative act we can take. But God still loves us, and seeks to restore us.

- Sin unravels God's creation, and so the natural consequence of choosing the path of sin is destruction.

- God is our Creator, not our destroyer.

- Even when God had every reason to deconstruct creation, God chose to re-create. God cannot stop being Creator—it's the nature of God.

- God will not leave us to our own devices. God promised to make our sin God's problem—to save us rather than destroy us. In Jesus Christ, God fulfilled this promise.

∾ NOTES

_____

_____

_____

_____

_____

_____

_____

_____

So here's what I want you to do, God helping you: Take your everyday, ordinary life—your sleeping, eating, going-to-work, and walking-around life—and place it before God as an offering. Embracing what God does for you is the best thing you can do for him. Don't become so well-adjusted to your culture that you fit into it without even thinking. Instead, fix your attention on God. You'll be changed from the inside out. Readily recognize what he wants from you, and quickly respond to it. Unlike the culture around you, always dragging you down to its level of immaturity, God brings the best out of you, develops well-formed maturity in you.

I'm speaking to you out of deep gratitude for all that God has given me, and especially as I have responsibilities in relation to you. Living then, as every one of you does, in pure grace, it's important that you not misinterpret yourselves as people who are bringing this goodness to God. No, God brings it all to you. The only accurate way to understand ourselves is by what God is and by what he does for us, not by what we are and what we do for him.

—Romans 12:1-3, TM

4 | *Clean*

⬬ INTRODUCTION

Even though we are designed to be God's image bearers, we are prone to focus on our own desires rather than God's desires. But every day is a new day, a fresh start. Even when our lives are a mess, the morning brings us another opportunity to turn toward God. And God has proven to be faithful, loving without limit, willing to take us back over and over and over again.

God wants us to be who we're made to be—worshipers of God—but God knows we can't without the Spirit's help. Without the *Ruach*, we can't be fully human. We even need God's help to repent! But remember: God didn't require us to make a promise; God made a promise to us.

And just as God recreated from the destruction and chaos of the flood, God can bring new life out of the damages and disorder of your mess—no matter how impossible or improbable it may seem to you.

๑๑ BREATHE IN THE WORD

Read each scripture passage and answer the question after the passage.

Psalm 51:1-2: What is your initial reaction to the boldness of David's prayer? Why?

Psalm 51:3-9: David has just committed adultery, impregnated another man's wife, and then had the husband killed to cover it up. What does he mean when he tells God "against you, you only, have I sinned"?

Psalm 51:10-12: We've been praying this prayer for several weeks now. How does seeing it in context change or enhance your understanding of David's words?

Psalm 51:13-19: If the only way David can worship God is if God opens David's lips, how does this impact the way you see yourself and what God expects of you?

∽

Creator God,
Breathe the Word of life into me.
Open my eyes to see beyond the words on the page.
Enliven my imagination to grasp the bigger story
you are still writing today.
May I surrender to the work you are doing
throughout history.
Right now, in this holy moment, create me anew.
In the name of Jesus and in the power of the Holy
Spirit,
Amen

Remember that we are looking at the Bible through the lens of biblical theology, asking God to open our eyes to the Spirit's echoes in scripture as we consider passages not as solitary stories but as open conversations that thread throughout the entire Bible. Remember, too, that we also bring ourselves to the conversation, and the way we see God affects how we read God's story. Ask God to open your eyes and your heart as you consider this week's passage.

{ # Psalm 51

What do you learn about the character of God?

What do you learn about what God is up to in our world?

How do you see this God at work in the world still today?

∞ EXERCISE

Have you ever felt like you've done something so terrible that you're unredeemable? Let's see how David's example could play out in our own lives.

- Find a room in your house where you can be undisturbed for a few moments. If there isn't a mirror already in that room, bring one with you. Same goes for a CD or MP3 player.

- Choose a word or phrase that describes the sin you're ashamed of (for example, if David were doing this exercise his labels would be: murderer and adulterer); write your word(s) on the mirror with a washable marker (or an eyeliner pencil or lipstick).

- Now, look in the mirror. Give yourself a few moments to just see your face with that label across it.

- Then, listen to the worship song "Beautiful Things" by Gungor. Don't sing along—just look at yourself and that label in the mirror and listen. When the song reaches the bridge and you hear the words "You are making me new," take a damp paper towel or washcloth and wipe the mirror clean.

- Play the song again. This time, ask God to help you sing along.

∾ REMEMBER

- God's character has been proven steadfast in love and mercy. Even when we don't deserve it, God can't help being God!

- Although we are made in God's image, we are free to choose not to fulfill our purpose. We need the help of God's Spirit to do what we are created for—to worship God.

- If we come before God offering nothing more than our brokenness, God will be faithful to give us a clean heart and a new spirit (the breath of God!).

- When we repent, we are fulfilling our purpose to worship God. The very act of turning back to God reveals our belief that God is who God says—loving and faithful and always creating and re-creating.

> Repentance is the way we participate in God's re-creation plan, by turning from sin and turning toward God.

⤳ MEDITATE

When it comes to putting broken lives back together—when it comes, in religious terms, to the saving of souls—the human best tends to be at odds with the holy best. To do for yourself the best that you have it in you to do—to grit your teeth and clench your fists in order to survive the world at its harshest and worst—is, by that very act, to be unable to let something be done for you and in you that is more wonderful still. The trouble with steeling yourself against the harshness of reality is that the same steel that secures your life against being destroyed secures your life also against being opened up and transformed by the holy power that life itself comes from. You can survive on your own. You can grow strong on your own. You can even prevail on your own. But you cannot become human on your own . . . what [we need] more than anything else in the world can be had only as a gift.[1]

—Frederick Buechner

⤳ NOTES

_____

_____

_____

_____

_____

5 | *Revive*

∾ INTRODUCTION

To be human is to worship, not to sin—remember that we were created to point creation back to the Creator. And sin doesn't just affect us on an individual level; sin spreads like a disease, infecting groups of people and entire nations. Throughout the Bible we see the Israelites turn away from God again and again, choosing instead the destructive trap of sin that works against God's good creation.

From what we've learned about the Creator, it makes sense that God forgives and helps those who are repentant, the ones who are trying to turn back to God and acknowledge that they need God. But what about the unrepentant ones, the people who are blatantly disregarding God's plan for humanity? Does it surprise you to find out that no matter what, God can't stop being Creator? Yes, even when we unapologetically run ourselves into the ground, God seeks to revive us, to breathe new life once again into the chaos and desolation, and to give us a new heart and a new spirit. Have you ever stopped to count the number of times Israel turns away from God, bent on destruction, and the number of times God revives them, breathing a new spirit into them? Don't forget that the main character of the Bible is God—and the life-giving, creative nature of God will always have the final word.

๑ BREATHE IN THE WORD

Read each scripture passage and answer the question after the passage.

Ezekiel 36:1-15: The nation of Israel is not repentant, yet God sends Ezekiel to tell them that in the midst of their well-deserved chaos and destruction, God promises to bring new life and a new future. What is your reaction to this news?

Ezekiel 36:16-32: How does this passage expand the image of God that Psalm 51 portrays?

Ezekiel 36:33-38: What does it mean to you that God is a rebuilder? Did you notice the complimentary reference to Eden? How is your worldview affected when you realize that God still considers the original plan for creation good?

Ezekiel 37:1-10: Why do you think God makes the restoration of the bones a two-part process, making life-giving breath a separate step? Does this clarify God's creation plan any further?

Ezekiel 37:11-14: How well do you think the people groups you are a part of (your family, your friends, your church, your nation) are bearing God's image? How does this passage encourage you?

∽ PRAYER

Creator God,
Breathe the Word of life into me.
Open my eyes to see beyond the words on the page.
Enliven my imagination to grasp the bigger story
you are still writing today.
May I surrender to the work you are doing
throughout history.
Right now, in this holy moment, create me anew.
In the name of Jesus and in the power of the
Holy Spirit,
Amen

Remember that we are looking at the Bible through the lens of biblical theology, asking God to open our eyes to the Spirit's echoes in scripture as we consider passages not as solitary stories but as open conversations that thread throughout the entire Bible. Remember, too, that we also bring ourselves to the conversation, and the way we see God affects how we read God's story. Ask God to open your eyes and your heart as you consider this week's passage.

{ Ezekiel 36:1—37:14

What do you learn about the character of God?

What do you learn about what God is up to in our world?

How do you see this God at work in the world still today?

౸ EXERCISE

Whether we live in a part of town that is outwardly in ruins, or an area that hides its desolation behind beautiful facades, our current world, including the very cities and neighborhoods we live in, is filled with the same brokenness that Israel experienced in Ezekiel's time. Let's see what God is up to today outside our own front doors.

- Set aside about twenty minutes to be outside in your neighborhood. Go on a walk if you're able to. If not, find a spot on your front porch/steps/balcony where you have a good view of your block.

- As you walk or sit, pay attention to what you see—people, buildings, nature. Observe the wind: Can you feel it? Can you see what it touches?

- Ask God to breathe new life into your neighborhood—to send the wind of the Spirit to restore the broken places. Be alert for signs of life.

- At the end of your time, write down anything that stood out to you (sights, smells, and feelings), no matter how insignificant or odd it may seem. Remember God works in unusual ways.

ᏇᎧ REMEMBER

- In our darkest hour, when chaos and destruction is all around, God can make all things new.

- Without God's Spirit living in us, we are apathetic—like the walking dead. But God's Spirit breathes new life into us.

- God wants to redeem whole groups of people, and God is at work even before people turn back and repent.

- Even when God's people go astray, God still has plans for their future.

ᏇᎧ NOTES

_____

_____

_____

_____

_____

_____

_____

_____

_____

◦◦ MEDITATE

The most experienced psychologist or observer of human nature knows infinitely less of the human heart than the simplest Christian who lives beneath the Cross of Jesus. The greatest psychological insight, ability, and experience cannot grasp this one thing: what sin is. Worldly wisdom knows what distress and weakness and failure are, but it does not know the godlessness of man. And so it also does not know that man is destroyed only by his sin and can be healed only by forgiveness. Only the Christian knows this. In the presence of a psychiatrist I can only be a sick man; in the presence of a Christian brother I can dare to be a sinner. The psychiatrist must first search my heart and yet he never plumbs its ultimate depth. The Christian brother knows when I come to him: here is a sinner like myself, a godless man who wants to confess and yearns for God's forgiveness. The psychiatrist views me as if there were no God. The brother views me as I am before the judging and merciful God in the Cross of Jesus Christ.[1]

—Dietrich Bonhoeffer

6 | *Word*

⤫ INTRODUCTION

In the Old Testament times, the Hebrew people understood the word as the Law, but in Jesus, the Word is revealed as a living, breathing person who is intimately involved with creation. Suddenly, God can be seen.

Emmanuel, God with us, is not a New Testament concept—from the very beginning God intended to dwell in creation. But after Adam and Eve unraveled God's Eden project, it isn't until Jesus comes to earth in human form that we get to tangibly see God dwelling in the world and begin to catch a clearer picture of God's plan for creation. In Jesus's very human birth and life, we see God make this world home, not merely a place to visit.

In Jesus, the world can see a complete picture of the Creator. And because Jesus both fully reflects God and perfectly embodies what it means to be human, we also finally have an example of who we were created to be as well.

As for the promise God made to Noah after the flood—Jesus, the Word of God, is the fulfillment of that promise. Not only does Jesus show us the way to God; he helps us to be reborn as God's children. The Word has come to make the old creation brand new!

⌒ BREATHE IN THE WORD

Read each scripture passage and answer the question after the passage.

John 1:1: Do you see the echoes of Genesis 1:1? How does this verse expand your view of the creation story?

John 1:2-5: How does the fact that *all things* came into being through Jesus impact your view of the world?

John 1:6-8: What if this was the definition of "human" in the dictionary? How would you see your life differently? How would your daily routine change?

John 1:9-13: How does what we've been learning the past few weeks expand what it means that we have "the right to become children of God . . . born of God?"

John 1:14-18: In Christ, we see a full and complete image of God. What does this reveal about God and God's image in you?

2 Corinthians 5:17: How do you want God to make you new? Or better yet, how do you think God wants to make you into a new creation?

⟶∽ PRAYER

Creator God,
Breathe the Word of life into me.
Open my eyes to see beyond the words on the page.
Enliven my imagination to grasp the bigger story
you are still writing today.
May I surrender to the work you are doing
throughout history.
Right now, in this holy moment, create me anew.
In the name of Jesus and in the power of the Holy
Spirit,
Amen

Remember that we are looking at the Bible through the lens of biblical theology, asking God to open our eyes to the Spirit's echoes in scripture as we consider passages not as solitary stories but as open conversations that thread throughout the entire Bible. Remember, too, that we also bring ourselves to the conversation, and the way we see God affects how we read God's story. Ask God to open your eyes and your heart as you consider this week's passage.

{ ## John 1:1-18

What do you learn about the character of God?

What do you learn about what God is up to in our world?

How do you see this God at work in the world still today?

❧ EXERCISE

In *The Message*, Eugene Peterson translates John 1:14 like this:

The Word became flesh and blood,
and moved into the neighborhood.

How would you view your life differently if you believed that God cared so much about humanity—about you!—that God sent Jesus to move into your neighborhood, to actively participate in your everyday life?

- Sit down with your schedule for the next week. Make a list of everything you plan to do over the next few days—the major events down to the most basic activities (wake up, shower, eat breakfast, do the dishes, sleep, and so on).

- Read over the list and highlight any activities you consider spiritual. Sit with this altered list for a moment.

- Now read each item on your list again and highlight each one after you read it—no matter what it is. Sit with your fully highlighted list of activities and consider what it means that God became human, that God dwells in this world with you, that your everyday activities aren't insignificant to God, and that God wants to bring new life to you every single day.

∽ REMEMBER

- The Word becoming flesh reminds us that God can speak to us through unlikely people and in unlikely places.

- Jesus is fully God. If you want to know what the unseen God looks like, take a look at the life, death, and resurrection of Jesus Christ.

- Because of Jesus, the law does not have the last word over us. Jesus is the only Word and he is full of grace and truth. God has always been loving and gracious—but Jesus is grace come down to where we can reach it.

- The darkness of the world cannot overcome the light of Christ.

How are you seeing God's creative work in the world today?

∾ MEDITATE

For grace to be grace, it must give us things we didn't know we needed and take us to places where we didn't want to go. As we stumble through the crazily altered landscape of our lives, we find that God is enjoying our attention as never before. And maybe that's the point. . . A way where there is no way; this is what God, and only God, can provide. This is salvation, which in Hebrew means widening or making sufficient. As we move from death to life we discover grace, a force as real as gravity, and are reminded of its presence in the changing of the seasons, and in the dying of seeds from which new life emerges, so that even our deserts may bloom.[1]

—Kathleen Norris

∾ NOTES

_____

_____

_____

_____

_____

_____

_____

7 Receive

∞ INTRODUCTION

The resurrection of Jesus is the climax of God's creation story, but unlike most story structures, God's climax doesn't come at the end; instead, it rises amid the chaos of history and affects everything—from beginning to end.

Jesus's life and death and resurrection prove to us, once and for all, that apart from God we cannot fulfill our purpose. But they also reveal to us the true nature of God—the steadfast, loving Creator who knew we couldn't even be human without God's help. In Jesus, we not only find our humanity; we become new humans living in a new creation that all points back to the Creator.

The resurrected Jesus still bore the scars of the destructive nature of sin. But in the resurrection all things are made new, even the things that sin had destroyed. And the crazy miracle is this: No longer is it God's creation that is being destroyed by sin; death doesn't have the last word anymore. Now it is sin that is being deconstructed by the resurrection of the Son; it is life that has the final say.

On the other side of resurrection, we are freed from the power of sin and given the gift of the Spirit. And not only do we get to be recipients of the Spirit; we are also given the gift of being participants in the Spirit's creative work in the world!

୬୬ BREATHE IN THE WORD

Read each scripture passage and answer the question after the passage.

John 20:1-10: Can you see the echoes of the creation story in verse 1? How does that change how you read this passage?

John 20:11-15: Mary doesn't recognize Jesus. In fact, she mistakes him for the gardener. How does this reflect back to the creation story?

John 20:16-18: Mary only recognizes Jesus when he calls her by her name. He gives her order and a place. What does this reveal about our relationship with God?

John 20:19-20: Why does Jesus show the disciples his scars? What does the fact that the resurrected Jesus still has scars signify to you?

John 20:21-23: What do we learn from this passage about what it means to be part of the post-resurrection new creation?

〜∽

∾ PRAYER

Creator God,
Breathe the Word of life into me.
Open my eyes to see beyond the words on the page.
Enliven my imagination to grasp the bigger story
you are still writing today.
May I surrender to the work you are doing
throughout history.
Right now, in this holy moment, create me anew.
In the name of Jesus and in the power of the
Holy Spirit,
Amen

Remember that we are looking at the Bible through the lens of biblical theology, asking God to open our eyes to the Spirit's echoes in scripture as we consider passages not as solitary stories but as open conversations that thread throughout the entire Bible. Remember, too, that we also bring ourselves to the conversation, and the way we see God affects how we read God's story. Ask God to open your eyes and your heart as you consider this week's passage.

{ John 20:1-23

What do you learn about the character of God?

What do you learn about what God is up to in our world?

How do you see this God at work in the world still today?

∾ EXERCISE

The resurrection of Jesus changes everything. Let us consider what this new creation we're invited into looks like.

- Gather the picture of yourself and the one of your loved one from your "Image" exercise a few weeks ago, as well as the container with the seed you planted during the "Promise" exercise (hopefully it's growing!).

- Find a comfy spot to sit where you have access to a CD or MP3 player.

- Listen to the song "New Wonders" by Sandra McCracken twice. The first time just listen as you look at the pictures and seedling, letting your thoughts roam. The second time pay attention to the words and perhaps even read along with the lyrics.

- When the song ends the second time, just sit in silence and pay attention to your breaths.

- Close your time in prayer, thanking God for what you're learning about the new creation revealed in Jesus Christ.

ᦔᧁ REMEMBER

- God will never stop bringing light into our darkness and speaking peace in the midst of our fear and chaos.

- After resurrection, Jesus was not a ghost, but a new human. He is the first to become a brand new creation. He is our hope!

- The resurrection of Christ is about more than forgiveness of sins—it is a new creation that we are invited to be part of.

- Through Christ we can receive the Holy Spirit and partner with God—experiencing the kingdom of God here and now and expanding its reach by sharing the grace we've been given.

> Being part of the new creation means being fully alive with the breath of God's Spirit.

∾ MEDITATE

We who live after Calvary and Easter know that God did indeed act suddenly and dramatically at that moment. When today we long for God to act, to put the world to rights, we must remind ourselves that he has already done so, and that what we are now awaiting is the full outworking of those events. We wait with patience, not like people in a dark room wondering if anyone will ever come with a lighted candle, but like people in early morning who know that the sun has arisen and are now waiting for the full brightness of midday.[1]

—N. T. Wright

∾ NOTES

_____

_____

_____

_____

_____

_____

_____

_____

Glossary

Create

- *Bara* (Hebrew): To create, shape, form. In the Old Testament this verb is only ever used to describe God's action.
- *Ruach* (Hebrew): Wind, breath, mind, spirit
- *Tov* (Hebrew): Good, fit for a purpose. Goodness is not defined by the opinions of others but by the design of God.

Image

- *Adam* (Hebrew): Human
- Image: Physical representation
- *Adamah* (Hebrew): Dirt, earth
- *Ish* (Hebrew): Male
- *Isha* (Hebrew): Female
- *Ezer Kenegdo* (Hebrew): Helper of great strength

Promise

- Sin: To make nothing out of something

Clean

- Hyssop: A shrub with healing and cleansing power

Word

- *Logos* (Greek): Word, thought, mind, worldview

Receive

- Resurrection: Receiving new life after death
- *Hagiazō* (Greek): To make holy
- Sanctification: Being fully alive in the Spirit, free from the destruction of sin

Notes

Chapter 1

1. C. S. Lewis, *Mere Christianity* (New York: Simon & Schuster, 1996), 176.

Chapter 2

1. Marilynne Robinson, *Gilead* (New York: Macmillan, 2005), 245-246.

Chapter 4

1. Frederick Buechner, *The Sacred Journey* (New York: HarperCollins, 1982), 46.

Chapter 5

1. Dietrich Bonhoeffer, *Life Together: The Classic Exploration of Faith in Community* (New York: Harper & Row, 1954).

Chapter 6

1. Kathleen Norris, *Acedia & Me: A Marriage, Monks, and a Writer's Life* (New York: Riverhead Books, 2010), 230, 285.

Chapter 7

1. N. T. Wright, *Matthew for Everyone, Part 1: Chapters 1-15* (Louisville: Westminster John Knox Press, 2004), 170.